From Your Friends At The MAILBOX®

Descriptive Writing!

Grades 4–6

Project Manager:
Thad H. McLaurin

Writer:
Carol A. Felts

Contributing Editor:
Scott Lyons

Art Coordinator:
Clevell Harris

Artists:
Nick Greenwood, Clevell Harris, Theresa Lewis, Rob Mayworth,
Rebecca Saunders, Donna K. Teal

Cover Artists:
Nick Greenwood and Kimberly Richard

www.themailbox.com

©2000 by THE EDUCATION CENTER, INC.
All rights reserved.
ISBN #1-56234-331-9

Manufactured in the United States

10 9 8 7 6 5 4 3

Table of Contents

About This Book

What Is Descriptive Writing?

In *descriptive writing,* a writer uses specific details and sensory words and phrases to develop images. A well-developed descriptive-writing selection contains an *introduction,* a *body,* and a *conclusion.* The *introduction* states the topic to be described in the body. The *body* includes specific details about the topic. The *conclusion* summarizes the information revealed in the body.

Develop and enhance your students' descriptive-writing skills with this easy-to-use collection of 20 two-page lessons. *Writing Works!—Descriptive* contains everything you need to supplement a successful writing program in your classroom.

Each two-page lesson contains the following:
- A motivating writing prompt
- Simple steps for teaching the prewriting and writing stages of each lesson
- A student reproducible that is either a graphic organizer used in the prewriting stages or a pattern on which students write their final drafts
- Suggestions for publishing or displaying students' work

Also included:
- A reproducible proofreading checklist for the student
- A reproducible descriptive-writing assessment for the teacher
- 16 extra descriptive-writing prompts
- A student reproducible containing 13 commonly used editing symbols

Other books in the Writing Works! series:
- *Writing Works!—Narrative*
- *Writing Works!—Explanatory*
- *Writing Works!—Clarification*
- *Writing Works!—Persuasive*
- *Writing Works!—Expressive*

What a Sight!

PROMPT *You're a tour guide at the local zoo and a reporter from the local newspaper wants to interview you about the three most popular sites or attractions at the zoo. Describe the three popular attractions so that the reporter can write her article.*

Think It!

1. Take a poll to see how many students have been to a zoo. Write on the board the names of the zoos visited by students. Then have students brainstorm different sites or attractions found at zoos. Also have students brainstorm what a visitor may see or hear at each site. List their responses on the board.

2. Give each student one copy of page 5. Then read aloud the prompt, display it on a transparency, or write it on the board.

3. Have each student select three zoo sites or attractions to describe. Then have her write the names of the three sites on the graphic organizer (page 5).

4. Direct the student to complete the organizer with words and phrases that describe the sights and sounds of each site.

Write It!

1. On the back of page 5 have each student write descriptive sentences using the words and phrases from her graphic organizer.
2. Direct the student to organize the information into three separate paragraphs— one for each site or attraction. Remind each student to begin the first paragraph with a topic sentence and end the last paragraph with a concluding sentence.
3. Encourage students to edit each other's work and make any needed corrections.
4. Have each student write the final version on another sheet of paper.
5. If desired, give each student one large sheet of construction paper and markers or crayons. Next, instruct the student to fold the paper in half. Have the student paste her writing inside the folded paper. Then instruct her to draw an illustration of one of the described sites on the front of the folded sheet of construction paper. Post the students' work around the classroom for all to enjoy.

Descriptive writing

TOPIC:
Sites at the Zoo

Subtopic
Zoo Site #1: _____

Details

Subtopic
Zoo Site #2: _____

Details

Subtopic
Zoo Site #3: _____

Details

Sunny Days

PROMPT

Think of a special or sunny day in your life. Maybe it was a special holiday, birthday, or just a great day that you enjoyed. Use the five Ws—Who? What? When? Where? Why?—to describe this very special day.

Describe for me, sir, a special day in your life.

Think It!

1. Share with your students a very special day in your life. Make sure your account includes the five Ws. Also include how this special day made you feel.

2. Have students brainstorm a list of special days. List their responses on the board.

3. Give each student a copy of page 7. Then read aloud the prompt above, display it on a transparency, or write the prompt on the board.

4. Instruct each student to think of a special day in his life. If a student is having trouble thinking of a special day, refer him to the list on the board to spark ideas.

5. Have each student record information related to the five Ws of his special day in the appropriate spaces on page 7.

Write It!

1. On the back of page 7, have each student write descriptive sentences using information recorded on the front of page 7.

2. Direct each student to organize his sentences into a complete descriptive paragraph, including a topic sentence and a concluding sentence.

3. Instruct the student to proofread and edit his work. Then have him write a final version of the paragraph on a separate sheet of paper. Remind the student to give his paragraph a title.

4. If desired, create the following display to showcase your students' work. Cover a bulletin board with red paper. Then tack several sheets of black poster board on the board. Have each student cut out his paragraph. Arrange the paragraphs on the sheets of poster board to resemble pages of a newspaper. Title the board "Extra! Extra! Sunny Days Abound!"

The Five Ws of Your Sunny Day

Title	
Who? (Who was a part of your special day?)	
What? (What happened on this special day?)	
When? (When was this special day?)	
Where? (Where did this special day take place?)	
Why? (Why was this day so special to you?)	

What a Dream!

You've just had the strangest dream! In your dream you shrank to the size of an ant for an entire day! Describe how things smelled, sounded, felt, looked, and/or tasted differently being so small. Also describe any dangers you encountered and how you were able to return to your normal size.

Think It!

1. Ask students if any of them have ever seen the movie *Honey, I Shrunk the Kids.* Then ask your students what happened to the kids in the story. *(A shrinking machine zapped them to sizes smaller than ants.)* Discuss with your students what it must be like to be that small. Have students brainstorm how being so small would make life difficult.

2. Read aloud the prompt above, display it on a transparency, or write it on the board. Then show your students the eraser end of a pencil. Have them imagine being no bigger than the eraser on the end of the pencil when thinking about their stories.

3. Give each student a copy of page 9. Have each student complete each dream bubble on the reproducible before beginning to write his story.

Write It!

1. Instruct each student to use the information recorded in each dream bubble on page 9 to help him write three paragraphs describing the dream: how things smelled, sounded, felt, looked, and/or tasted differently; dangers encountered; and how the student returned to normal size. Remind the student to have a topic sentence and concluding sentence for each paragraph.

2. Allow students time to proofread their work. Next, have students pair up to edit each other's paragraphs. Then instruct each student to write the final version of his story on a separate sheet of paper.

3. For a display, have each student glue his final copy onto the center of a 9" x 12" sheet of light blue construction paper. Then have him trim the outer edges of the construction paper to resemble a dream bubble. Next, give each student a sheet of drawing paper and crayons. Instruct each student to draw a picture of himself sleeping. Post each student's final copy/dream bubble on a bulletin board covered with black bulletin board paper and titled "What a Dream!" Next, post each student's illustration underneath his dream bubble. Tack cotton balls leading from the illustration to the dream bubble to simulate dreaming.

Name _____

What a Dream!

How things smelled, sounded, felt, looked, and/or tasted:

How you returned to your normal size:

Dangers you encountered:

En Route!

Describe the route you take to school beginning from your doorstep at home to the school's entrance. Also include specific details about two landmarks or sites you see along the way, such as a monument, an unusual building, a bridge, or a lake.

Think It!

1. Take a poll of your students to see how many walk, ride a bus, or ride in a car to school. Then describe the route you travel to school each day and the mode of transportation you take.

2. As you explain your daily route to school, draw a diagram of the route on the board. Mention some of the sites you see along the way and mark them on your diagram.

3. Read aloud the prompt above, display it on a transparency, or write it on the board. Then have each student sketch out on a sheet of scrap paper a map of her route from home to school. Instruct students to label as many streets and landmarks as they can remember.

4. Inform your students that their homework assignment is to check their maps for accuracy on their way home from school. Remind students to add any landmarks or street names they could not remember to make the maps as accurate as possible.

5. Have students return their maps the following day.

Write It!

1. Give each student a copy of page 11. Have each student use the sketch of her home-to-school route to create a detailed map in the box at the top of the reproducible. Then have the student record in the two boxes at the bottom of the page any details about two sites or landmarks she passes each day on her way to school.

2. Once a student has completed page 11, have her turn the page over to begin a rough draft of directions describing how to get from her home to the school. Instruct the student to include specific directions in the first paragraph. Then have her include details about the first site or landmark in the second paragraph, and details about the second site or landmark in the third paragraph. Remind students that each paragraph should contain a topic sentence and a concluding sentence.

3. Have each student proofread, edit, and revise her work before writing a final version on a clean sheet of paper.

4. Cover a bulletin board with black paper. Use yellow chalk to draw a horizontal dotted line across the middle of the board to simulate a road. Title the board "En Route."

5. Staple students' maps to the top half of the road. Then mix up the directions and staple them to the bottom half of the road. Encourage students to spend their free time trying to match each map to the correct set of directions.

En Route!

Directions: Draw and label a detailed map of the route you take each day from home to school. Label street names and sites or landmarks along your route. Include any map symbols in the Map Key box.

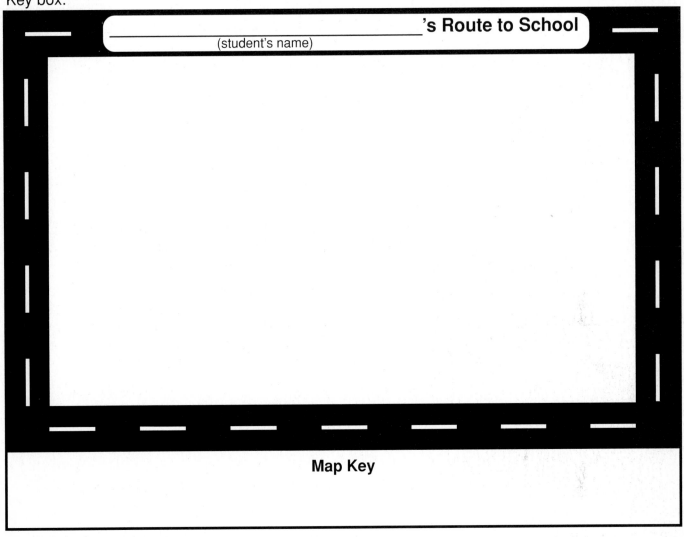

_____ **'s Route to School**
(student's name)

Map Key

Directions: List details about two sites or landmarks you pass on your way to school each morning.

Site/Landmark #1	**Site/Landmark #2**
_____	_____
(name)	(name)
Details: _____	**Details:** _____
_____	_____
_____	_____
_____	_____
_____	_____

Welcome Home!

Imagine your dream house. Choose a favorite room and describe what it looks like so that someone reading your paper could visualize it.

Think It!

1. Have students close their eyes while you orally describe a favorite place, such as a restaurant or an outdoor location. Be very detailed with your description. Have students open their eyes; then call on volunteers to recall specific words or phrases that helped them to visualize the place you described.

2. Give each student one copy of page 13. Then, read the prompt above, display it on a transparency, or write it on the board.

3. Challenge each student to draw a detailed picture of his favorite dream-house room on the pattern at the top of the page.

4. Have the student complete the web with words and phrases that describe the room using the five senses. Remind students to use sensory words similar to those you used in your description.

Write It!

1. On the back of his sheet, have each student write descriptive sentences using the words and phrases from his web.

2. Direct the student to organize his sentences into a complete descriptive paragraph, including a topic sentence and concluding sentence. Instruct the student to proofread and edit his work carefully. Encourage students to swap papers to peer-edit. After all corrections have been made, have the student write his paragraph on a separate sheet of paper.

3. If desired, have each student cut out his illustration and paragraph and paste them onto a colorful sheet of 12" x 18" construction paper. Display the completed projects on a bulletin board titled "Welcome Home!"

Welcome Home!

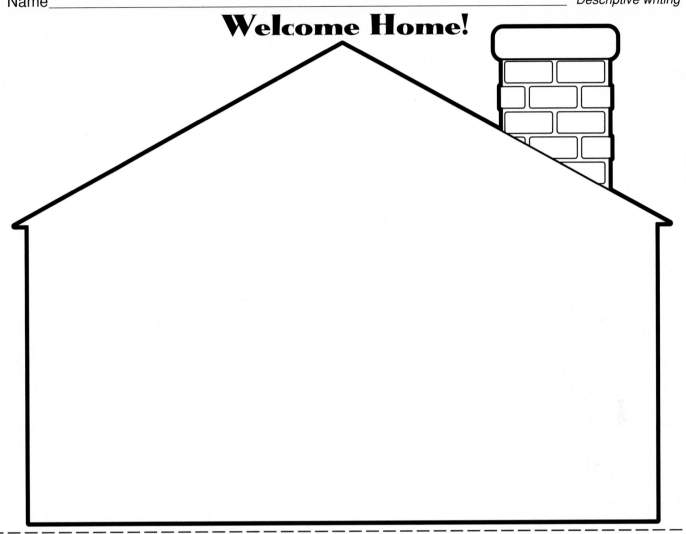

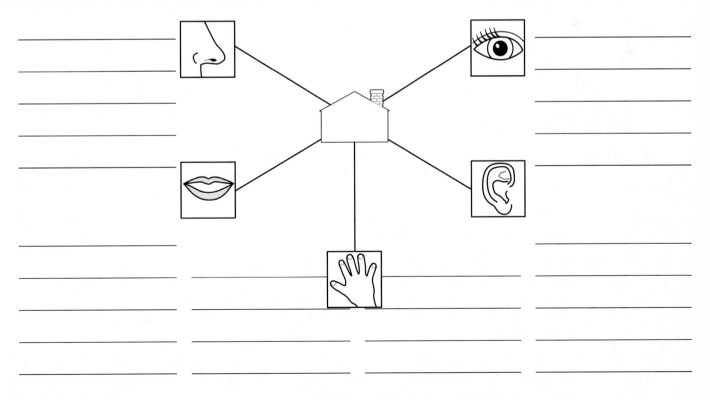

Parade of News

PROMPT *As a local television reporter, you've been assigned to report on the town's Fourth of July parade. Write a report describing the beginning, middle, and end of the parade.*

Think It!

1. Take a poll to see how many of your students have been to a parade. Discuss some of the things they saw, as well as the time of year the parade took place and the purpose of the parade.

2. Continue the discussion by asking what kinds of things might be seen in a Fourth of July parade. *(marching bands, patriotic floats, people in costumes, fire trucks)* List their responses on the board.

3. Read aloud the prompt above, display it on a transparency, or write it on the board. Then give each student a copy of page 15. Instruct each student to pretend that she is a reporter at the parade and page 15 is her clipboard on which to record details about what she sees.

Write It!

1. Inform each student that she will use the details she listed on page 15 to help her write the report of the parade for the next newscast.

2. Direct the student to proofread and edit her work carefully. Encourage students to swap papers for peer editing. After all corrections have been made, have the student write the final copy on another sheet of paper.

3. Conclude the activity by setting up a table with a real or pretend microphone. Then have each student read her report of the parade as if she were a newscaster on the six o'clock news.

Directions: Fill in the clipboard below with details about the beginning, middle, and end of the Fourth of July parade you're covering for the six o'clock news.

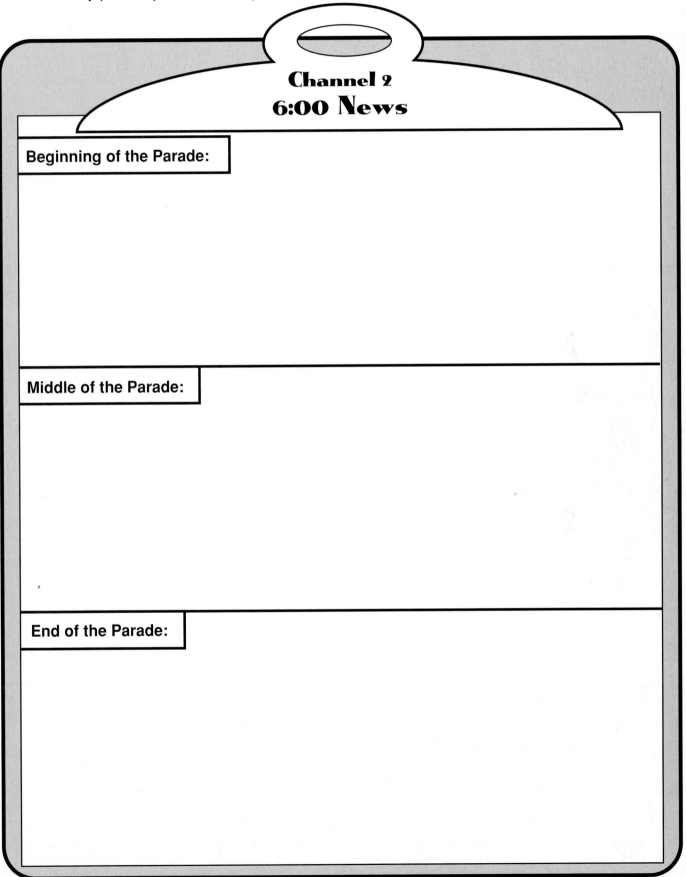

Channel 2
6:00 News

Beginning of the Parade:

Middle of the Parade:

End of the Parade:

Picture-Perfect

You've just returned from an exciting tropical island vacation. The pictures of your trip were damaged. Write a letter to your pen pal, describing the beautiful scenery so vividly that he can picture it in his mind.

Think It!

1. Ask your students to think a moment about their last vacation or trip. Discuss briefly where they went and what they did. List some of the places visited by students on the board.

2. Continue the discussion by talking with students about what kinds of pictures are usually taken on a vacation *(landmarks, scenery, family members, places of interest, wildlife, etc.)*.

3. Read aloud the prompt above, display it on a transparency, or write it on the board. Have students brainstorm a list of things that might be found on the beach of a tropical island *(a hut, white sand, shells, a palm tree, blue water, birds, a crab, boats, etc.)*. List their responses on the board.

4. Give each student a sheet of drawing paper and crayons. Instruct the student to use his imagination to draw the scene of the tropical island beach that he's going to describe in the letter to his pen pal.

Write It!

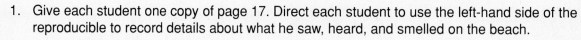

1. Give each student one copy of page 17. Direct each student to use the left-hand side of the reproducible to record details about what he saw, heard, and smelled on the beach.

2. Then instruct each student to use his illustration and the details recorded on page 17 as a guide to help him write a rough draft of the friendly letter describing the scene to his pen pal.

3. Direct the student to proofread and edit his work carefully. Encourage students to swap papers to peer-edit. After all corrections have been made, have the student write the final copy of his friendly letter on the right-hand side of page 17.

4. Display each student's letter and illustration on a bulletin board titled "Picture-Perfect." Decorate the board with fishing net, shells, shovels, and buckets.

Descriptive writing

Dear Pen Pal,

_____

_____

_____

_____

_____

Your friend,

_____
(signature)

What I saw: _____

What I heard: _____

What I smelled: _____

Very Special People

Think of a very special person you know. Describe the qualities that make this person so special.

Think It!

1. Have your students close their eyes and think about the different people in their lives. Suggest to students that they may be thinking of their moms, dads, grandparents, cousins, neighbors, teachers, friends, etc. Then ask each student to think of a person she considers to be very special.

2. Have student volunteers share the special person that came to mind. List their responses on the board. Then read aloud the prompt above, display it on a transparency, or write it on the board.

3. Give each student a copy of page 19. Instruct the student to write the name of her special person in the center of the page and draw an illustration of the special person in the oval above the name. Next, have the student complete the rest of the reproducible with details and information about the special person.

Write It!

1. Direct each student to use the details she listed in the boxes on page 19 to write four paragraphs about her special person. Remind the student to begin each paragraph with a topic sentence and end each sentence with a concluding sentence.

2. Direct the student to proofread and edit her work carefully. Encourage students to swap papers to peer-edit. After all corrections have been made, have the student write the final copy on another sheet of paper.

3. Display students' work by posting the writings outside your classroom door for all to enjoy. Title the display "The Special People in Our Lives."

Very Special People

Physical traits:

_____

_____

_____

_____

_____

_____

_____

Personality traits:

_____

_____

_____

_____

_____

_____

_____

My Very Special Person

_____
(name)

One special way this person has helped me:

_____

_____

_____

_____

_____

_____

_____

One special way this person has helped others:

_____

_____

_____

_____

_____

_____

_____

All in a Day's Work

PROMPT *Your class is preparing a time capsule to be opened in 50 years. Your job is to write a description of a typical day in school for the time capsule. Include in the description your schedule, equipment and supplies used, and special events attended.*

Glenview School 2000

Think It!

1. Ask your students to imagine what school will be like in 50 years. List their responses on the board.

2. Read aloud the prompt above, display it on a transparency, or write it on the board.

3. Write the start time for school at the top of the board. Then write the end time for school at the bottom of the board. Have your students help you brainstorm a list of events that occur during a typical day at school. Write their responses on the board in between the two times listed.

Write It!

1. Give each student one copy of page 21. Instruct each student to use page 21 and the events listed on the board to help them construct a schedule of a typical school day.

2. After each student has completed page 21, post the time-order words listed below on the board or a sheet of chart paper, or display them on a transparency. Explain that using such words and phrases can help them better describe the events of a typical day in the order that they occur.

after	before long	immediately	meanwhile
afterward	earlier	instantly	next
at the same time	finally	just as	soon
before	first	last	then
	for a moment	later	until

3. Have each student use the information recorded on page 21 and the time-order words listed above to write his description of a typical school day for the time capsule.

4. Direct the student to proofread and edit his work carefully. Encourage students to swap papers to peer-edit. After all corrections have been made, have the student write the final copy on another sheet of paper.

5. Display each student's work on a bulletin board covered with black paper and titled "Remember When?" To give the board a futuristic look, decorate it with star, moon, and spaceship shapes cut from aluminum foil.

DAILY SCHEDULE

TIME	ACTIVITY

Toying Around With New Ideas

PROMPT

Tuttle Toy Company, Inc., has announced a new toy contest! They are looking for the perfect toy designed for kids by a kid. Describe the toy idea you plan to submit. You can describe a brand-new toy or an improvement to an existing toy.

Think It!

1. Have your students brainstorm a list of their favorite toys. Then call on student volunteers to explain what about the particular toys listed makes them so special or fun to play.

2. Read aloud the prompt above, display it on a transparency, or write it on the board.

3. Give each student one copy of page 23. Then have each student think of an idea for a new toy or an idea for how to improve an existing toy.

4. Instruct the student to draw an illustration of the new toy in the box provided at the top of page 23. Then have the student complete the descriptive word webs at the bottom of the page.

Write It!

1. Have each student use the illustration and the information she records in the word webs on page 23 to help her write two descriptive paragraphs about her new toy.

2. Direct the student to proofread and edit her work carefully. Encourage students to swap papers to peer-edit. After all corrections have been made, have the student write the final copy on another sheet of paper.

3. Display the students' writing on a bulletin board titled "Toying Around With New Ideas!" For a decorative touch, post magazine pictures of various toys around the board.

Toying Around With New Ideas!

Directions: In the box below, draw an illustration of your new or newly improved toy. Then complete each word web at the bottom of the page by filling in descriptive words or phrases that describe or give details about each topic box.

Name of Toy: _____

Descriptive Word Webs

**TOPIC
What the Toy Looks Like**

**TOPIC
How the Toy Can Be Used**

Serious Cereal

PROMPT

There are dozens of breakfast cereals on the market today. They contain anything from nuts and whole grains to sugar and candy. You've been hired to create a new cereal. Write a descriptive paragraph about your new cereal as it might appear on the back of the cereal box.

Think It!

1. In advance, have each student bring in one empty breakfast cereal box.

2. On the day of this writing activity, display several of the cereal boxes in front of your class for all to see. Then select a few boxes and read aloud the descriptions of the cereals (usually found on the side or back of the box).

3. Have students help you list all the descriptive words used to describe the cereals *(crunchy, complete, fortified, healthy, tasty, etc.).*

4. Read aloud the prompt above, display it on a transparency, or write it on the board.

5. Inform each student that he is going to create the latest breakfast cereal to be introduced on the market. Further explain that in order to sell the product, he has to write a descriptive paragraph about his new product that will be printed on the cereal box.

Write It!

1. Give each student a copy of page 25. Then instruct the student to complete the word webs on the reproducible by writing a different word in each circle that describes the topic in each box.

2. Instruct each student to use the completed word webs to write a descriptive paragraph about his cereal's taste, texture, nutrition, and uniqueness.

3. Direct the student to proofread and edit his work carefully. Encourage students to swap papers to peer-edit. After all corrections have been made, have the student write the final copy on another sheet of paper.

4. If desired, supply each student with several sheets of construction paper, scissors, glue, and crayons. Instruct the student to cover his cereal box with construction paper. Then have him glue his descriptive paragraph to the front of the box. Next, have him decorate the rest of the box with the name of his cereal and illustrations of his cereal.

5. Tack each student's decorated cereal box to a bulletin board titled "Serious Cereal."

Serious Cereal

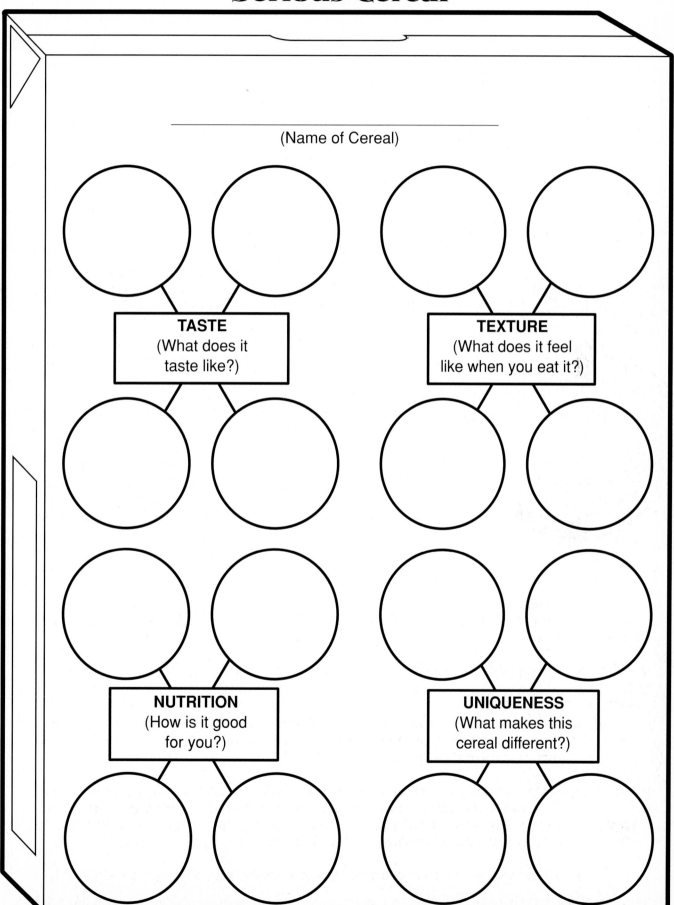

_____
(Name of Cereal)

TASTE
(What does it
taste like?)

TEXTURE
(What does it feel
like when you eat it?)

NUTRITION
(How is it good
for you?)

UNIQUENESS
(What makes this
cereal different?)

"Just the Facts, Ma'am"

PROMPT

Imagine that you've witnessed a minor automobile accident. When the police arrive, an officer hands you a form and asks you to describe exactly what you saw. She wants all the facts.

Think It!

1. Poll students to discover if any of them have ever seen an automobile accident. Select a few student volunteers to briefly describe what they saw. Then brainstorm with the class a list of synonyms for *accident.* List their responses on the board. *(Possible responses: mishap, disaster, emergency, misadventure, calamity)*

2. Give each child a copy of page 27. Then read aloud the prompt above, display it on a transparency, or write it on the board.

3. Before the students begin writing their eyewitness reports, encourage them to think about what the automobiles look like, and what each vehicle did that led up to the collision. Stress to your students the importance of thinking of as many details as possible.

4. After visualizing the crash and the vehicles involved, have each child illustrate the official "photograph" of the accident in the box provided at the top of page 27. Then, on the back of the reproducible, direct each child to list exactly what happened, in the order that it happened.

Write It!

1. Using the information from his list and the official "photograph" as a reference, have each student begin writing his report. Remind him to use order words—such as *first, next,* and *then*—when writing up his report. Also encourage each child to use some of the class-brainstormed synonyms for *accident.*

2. Have students pair up to edit and review each other's "photographs" and reports, checking for details and errors. The police report needs to be as accurate as possible.

3. To create an arresting display with these reports, give each student a manila folder—his case file. Have him glue his police report inside the file. Then write a different case number on the outside of each folder (Case #001, Case #002, etc.) to make them look like official police reports. Mount their reports on a bulletin board titled "Just the Facts, Ma'am" in a way that allows the folders to be easily opened and read by all.

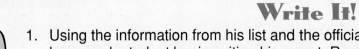

"Just the Facts, Ma'am"

Police Report

(Photograph of the Accident After It Occurred)

Name of Witness: _____

Date and Time of Accident: _____

Location of Accident:_____

Eyewitness Report

_____

_____

_____

_____

_____

_____

_____

_____

_____

_____

_____

_____

_____

_____

_____
Signature and Date

High in the Sky

PROMPT

As a birthday gift, you received a free hot-air balloon ride. Describe what you saw on your ride in the sky. Also describe what it felt like to be so high in the sky.

Think It!

1. Ask for a show of hands of any students who've ever ridden in an airplane before. Then have a few student volunteers describe what it felt like to ride in a plane. Also have the students share with the rest of the class what they saw so far up in the sky.

2. Read aloud the prompt above, display it on a transparency, or write it on the board. Then explain to students that a hot-air balloon ride takes a person high in the sky, but that objects on the ground can still be seen.

3. Have each student close his eyes. Instruct him to select a location for his balloon ride to begin (his home, school, the beach, the mountains, etc.). Next, tell him to imagine that he is slowly lifting off the ground in a hot-air balloon. Tell him to imagine the objects he sees below.

4. Have him open his eyes and list on a sheet of paper some of the sites he has flown over during his balloon ride.

Write It!

1. Give each student a copy of page 29. Also ask the student to get out a sheet of notebook paper.

2. Instruct the student to write, on the sheet of notebook paper, three descriptive paragraphs about his ride. Have him use the topic sentences starters listed on page 29 as the first sentences in each paragraph.

3. Remind the student that the sentences within each paragraph should be details only about that paragraph's topic.

4. Direct the student to proofread and edit his work carefully. Encourage students to swap papers to peer-edit. After all corrections have been made, have the student write the final copy on his copy of page 29.

5. After each student has completed his final writing, have him lightly color and then cut out the balloon pattern on page 29. Mount each balloon on a colored sheet of construction paper. Then use string to hang each student's balloon writing from the ceiling around the classroom.

High in the Sky

When my hot-air balloon ride first began, I saw _____

_____

_____

_____

_____

Next, I saw _____

_____

_____

_____

_____

As we landed, I could see _____

_____

_____

_____

_____

_____

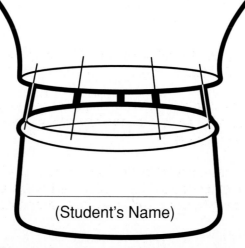

_____
(Student's Name)

Out of This World!

You've just returned from an exploratory mission to the moon. While there you encountered a friendly group of aliens. NASA wants a full descriptive report of your mission.

Think It!

1. Write *astronaut* in large letters on the board. Then have students help you list all the words that come to mind when they see that word *(space, moon, rocket, alien, shuttle, Mars, etc.)*.

2. Read aloud the prompt above, display it on a transparency, or write it on the board. Then explain to your students that *NASA* stands for National Aeronautics and Space Administration and that it is a government agency that controls all U.S. missions into space.

3. Give each student a copy of page 31. Instruct each student to use the reproducible to organize her thoughts for her final report to NASA.

Write It!

1. Direct each student to use the information she records on page 31 to write a four-paragraph, detailed report to NASA. Inform the student that there should be one paragraph for each topic listed on page 31. Remind the student that each paragraph should have a topic sentence.

2. Direct the student to proofread and edit her work carefully. Encourage students to swap papers to peer-edit. After all corrections have been made, have the student write the final copy on another sheet of paper.

3. If desired, give each student one sheet of drawing paper and crayons. Have the student illustrate one scene from her mission. Attach each student's report to one side of a large sheet of black construction paper; then attach her illustration to the other side. Have the student use yellow or white chalk to decorate the borders of the black construction paper with moons and stars. Use string to hang the writings/illustrations around the classroom for all to enjoy.

MISSION REPORT

Topic #1	Topic #2	Topic #3	Topic #4
What happened upon first landing on the moon?	How did you discover the aliens?	What did the aliens look like?	How did the encounter end?
Details:	Details:	Details:	Details:
1. _____	1. _____	1. _____	1. _____
2. _____	2. _____	2. _____	2. _____
3. _____	3. _____	3. _____	3. _____
4. _____	4. _____	4. _____	4. _____
5. _____	5. _____	5. _____	5. _____

Lost Luggage

PROMPT *You have just arrived at your vacation destination, and you find out the airline has lost a piece of your luggage. The airline has asked you to write a description of the piece of luggage and its contents.*

Think It!

1. Ask each student to think of a favorite vacation. Have a few student volunteers share the locations of their favorite vacations. Then ask if anyone has ever arrived at a vacation spot to discover that his luggage is lost. Have student volunteers share their experiences.

2. Read aloud the prompt above, display it on a transparency, or write it on the board.

3. Give each student one copy of page 33. Then ask each student to think of a piece of luggage he has at home (or he can make up a piece of luggage). Instruct the student to complete the reproducible to help him organize his thoughts before writing his description of the missing luggage and contents for the airline.

Write It!

1. Instruct each student to use the data he recorded on page 33 to help him begin a draft of the three-paragraph description he's going to submit to the airline.

2. Direct the student to proofread and edit his work carefully. Encourage students to swap papers to peer-edit. After all corrections have been made, have the student write the final copy on another sheet of paper.

3. To display student writing, try one of the following suggestions:
   - In advance, have each student bring in one shoebox with its lid. Have each student decorate his box to resemble his missing piece of luggage. Instruct the student to attach his descriptive writing to the front of his "suitcase." Display them around the room for all to enjoy.
   - Bring in several suitcases. (Ask parent volunteers to supply a few.) Attach four or five student writings to the front of each suitcase. Display the suitcases underneath the heading "Lost Luggage."

Name

Lost Luggage

Details about what the missing luggage looks like:

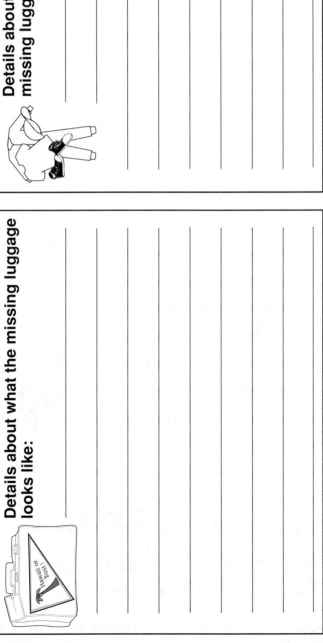

Details about clothing inside the missing luggage:

Details about other items inside the missing luggage:

The Mysterious Door

PROMPT

After school one day, you return to your class for a book and notice a mysterious door! You open the door and discover it takes you to a magical land. Describe what you see, hear, smell, and feel behind the mysterious door.

Think It!

1. Have your students think of imaginary places they've read about in books or seen in movies or on television, such as Narnia, the settings for Dr. Seuss books, and the Hundred Acre Wood. Have students explain why such places couldn't really exist.

2. Read aloud the prompt above, display it on a transparency, or write it on the board.

3. Give each student one copy of page 35. Instruct each student to use page 35 to help him organize his thoughts and record details about what he sees, hears, smells, and feels behind the mysterious door.

Write It!

1. Instruct each student to write four descriptive paragraphs about her experience behind the mysterious door—one paragraph for each topic on page 35. Remind students to have a topic sentence and concluding sentence for each paragraph.

2. Direct the student to proofread and edit her work carefully. Encourage students to swap papers to peer-edit. After all corrections have been made, have the student write the final copy on another sheet of paper.

3. Give each student a large sheet of white construction paper. Have the student fold it in half like a book cover. Instruct the student to illustrate the magic door on the front of the cover. Then have the student paste her descriptive writing on the inside (right-hand side) of the cover. Display each student's work on and around your classroom door with the heading "The Mysterious Door."

The Mysterious Door

What I saw: _____

_____
_____
_____
_____
_____
_____
_____
_____
_____
_____
_____
_____

What I heard: _____

_____
_____
_____
_____
_____
_____
_____
_____
_____
_____
_____
_____

What I smelled: _____

_____
_____
_____
_____
_____
_____
_____
_____
_____

What I felt: _____

_____
_____
_____
_____
_____
_____
_____
_____
_____

Animal Discovery

You are on an African photo safari when you discover an animal that no one has ever seen before! It looks like a combination of two existing animals. You decide to track it. Describe what it looks like, what it eats, and where it lives.

Hello, I'm a lyena.

Think It!

1. Show your students a world map and have them locate the continent of Africa. Then explain to them that a photo *safari* is a trip to see and photograph wild animals. Have your students help you list animals that make their homes in Africa, such as lions, elephants, and hyenas.

2. Read aloud the prompt above, display it on a transparency, or write it on the board.

3. Use the following example to show students how two animals might be combined to create the new animal discovered:
   Example: lion + hyena = lyena or hion

4. Give each student one copy of page 37. Have the student use page 37 to help her organize her thoughts for three descriptive paragraphs about her new discovery.

Write It!

1. Instruct the student to write a rough draft of her description on the back of page 37.

2. Direct the student to proofread and edit her work carefully. Encourage students to swap papers to peer-edit. After all corrections have been made, have the student write the final copy on another sheet of paper.

3. Give each student a large sheet of drawing paper and crayons. Instruct the student to write the name of her new animal discovery at the top of the sheet. Then have her illustrate the creature on the rest of the sheet. Staple the student's writing to the bottom of the illustration; then post all the writings on a board titled "On Safari."

Descriptive writing

Animal Discovery

_____
(Name of animal)

Where It Lives

→ **Details**

What It Eats

→ **Details**

What It Looks Like

→ **Details**

Kitchen Gadgets Galore!

PROMPT *Kitchens are full of gadgets of all shapes and sizes, each with a different way to make life simpler. Choose one such item to examine and describe in detail.*

Think It!

1. Write *gadget* on the board. Explain to your students that this term is often used to refer to small mechanical or electronic devices that have practical uses. Then have students help you make a list of common gadgets found in the kitchen: electric mixer, food processor, food scale, can opener, etc.

2. Read aloud the prompt above, display it on a transparency, or write it on the board.

3. Have each student select one of the gadgets listed on the board. Then give each student one copy of page 39. Instruct the student to complete the reproducible by filling in the appropriate boxes with details about the selected kitchen gadget.

Write It!

1. After the student has completed page 39, have her use the details to write (on the back of the reproducible) four detailed, descriptive paragraphs about the gadget. Before the student begins writing, however, tell her to describe the selected gadget without revealing the gadget's name.

2. Direct the student to proofread and edit her work carefully. Encourage students to swap papers to peer-edit. After all corrections have been made, have the student write the final copy on another sheet of paper.

3. After each student has completed the final version of her description, have the student swap papers with another student and try to guess the other student's gadgets based on the descriptions.

4. Display each student's final writing and graphic organizer (page 39) on a bulletin board covered with a red-and-white checkered tablecloth. Title the board "Kitchen Gadgets Galore!" If desired, hang kitchen utensils—such as spoons, forks, spatulas, and hand mixers—around the border of the bulletin board.

Kitchen Gadgets Galore!

What does this gadget look like? | **What does this gadget sound like?**

_____
_____
_____
_____
_____
_____
_____
_____
_____
_____
_____
_____
_____

Draw an illustration of your gadget here.

_____
(name of gadget)

What is the purpose of this gadget? | **How does this gadget save time?**

Amazing Amusement Parks

PROMPT

You've just been chosen to design a brochure for the newest amusement park in America! Choose three of the park's best features—such as rides, shows, games, or food—to describe in your brochure.

Scream Machine 2000

Think It!

1. In advance collect several brochures for different attractions in your state or from around the country. AAA (the American Automobile Association®) is a good source for such material.

2. Pass the brochures around for all your students to see. Then discuss with your students the characteristics of brochures. *(They usually list just the major aspects of a site, not every detail. They highlight the site's most attractive qualities, and are usually very colorful and eye-catching.)*

3. Read aloud the prompt above, display it on a transparency, or write it on the board.

4. Brainstorm with your students the different areas that might be found in an amusement park, such as rides, places to eat, games, shows, etc.

Write It!

1. Instruct each student to get out one sheet of notebook paper. Then have the student fold the sheet into three equal sections like a brochure. Next have her unfold the sheet and lay it flat on her desk.

2. Direct the student to label the tops of the folded sections with the names of the three amusement park areas she's selected to describe in her brochure. Then instruct the student to use the space below each heading to write a rough draft of the brochure, including as many details as possible.

3. Direct the student to proofread and edit her work carefully. Encourage students to swap papers to peer-edit. After all corrections have been made, give the student a copy of page 41 on which to write and illustrate her final copy.

4. Display the student-made brochures on a bulletin board titled "Amazing Amusement Parks!"

_____ (Name of Amusement Park)

(Name of First Area) _____

(Draw illustration here.)

_____

(Name of Second Area) _____

_____

(Draw illustration here.)

(Name of Third Area) _____

(Draw illustration here.)

_____

Created by _____

Mean Cuisine

PROMPT

Think about all of the foods you like to eat. Which is your favorite? Describe your favorite food so that someone who reads your words can just about taste how delicious it is.

Think It!

1. Have each student take out a sheet of paper and list all of his favorite foods.

2. Read aloud the prompt above, display it on a transparency, or write it on the board. Then tell each student to choose one favorite food from his list and circle it. Keep track of the class's favorites by tallying them on the board as the students relay them to you.

Write It!

1. Have each student fold another sheet of paper in half, then in half again, forming four equal-sized squares. Instruct the student to label one square "Sounds," one "Preparation," another "When," and the last "Picture."

2. Tell each student that in the "Sounds" box, he is to list all of the sounds associated with his favorite food, both from making it and eating it. In the "Preparation" box, instruct the student to describe who cooks or makes his favorite food and how it is prepared. The "When" box should contain details about how often the student eats the favorite food. Last, the "Picture" box should have a sketch of the ready-to-eat food.

3. Instruct the student to flip the sheet of paper over. Direct the student to organize the information from the front (except the illustration) into paragraphs, having one paragraph for each of the three boxes of information. Remind the student that each paragraph should contain a topic and concluding sentence.

4. Direct the student to proofread and edit his work carefully. Encourage students to swap papers to peer-edit.

5. Give each student one copy of page 43, scissors, crayons, string, and one paper plate. After all corrections have been made, have the student write the final copy on the recipe card on page 43. Then instruct the student to cut out the card and set it aside. Next have the student draw and color an illustration of his favorite food on the paper plate. Using a hole puncher, have each student punch a hole in the top of his card and in the bottom of the paper plate. Attach the two pieces with string and display them on a board titled "Mean Cuisine."

My Favorite Food

_____
(Name of Food)

_____

_____

_____

_____

_____

_____

_____

_____

_____

_____

_____

_____

by: _____

Proofreading Checklist

To the Student: Use this checklist during the proofreading or editing stage of your writing to help you determine what needs improving and/or correcting before writing the final version. Then give this checklist and your writing to a peer editor (a classmate) to use to edit your work.

Title of Writing Selection:_____

Things to Check	Writer's Checklist		Peer Editor's Checklist	
	Yes	No	Yes	No
1. Does the writing have an introduction, a body, and a conclusion?				
2. Does the writing make sense and is it easy to read?				
3. Did the writer use descriptive words?				
4. Does each sentence begin with a capital letter?				
5. Does each sentence have an ending punctuation mark?				
6. Did the writer use complete sentences?				
7. Did the writer check for misspelled words?				
8. Is each paragraph indented?				
9. Does each paragraph contain a topic sentence?				
10. Does each paragraph contain a concluding sentence?				
11. Do all the details stick to the topic?				

☆ If the peer editor checked "No" in any box above, discuss it with the editor.

Think About It!

I think I did a _____ job on this writing selection because…

_____

_____

Descriptive-Writing Assessment

Student's Name: _____ **Date:** _____

Title of Writing: _____

Assessment Items	Agree	Disagree
1. Descriptive words and sensory details are used.		
2. The writing selection makes sense; it is easy to read.		
3. The writing selection has an introduction, a body, and a conclusion.		
4. Information and details are presented in a logical order.		
5. All details relate to the topic.		
6. Correct punctuation is used.		
7. Each sentence begins with a capital letter.		
8. Each word is spelled correctly.		
9. Run-on sentences and incomplete sentences are avoided.		
10. Each paragraph contains a topic sentence.		
11. Each paragraph contains a concluding sentence.		
12. Each verb agrees with its subject.		
13. All proper nouns are capitalized.		
14. Each paragraph is indented.		
15. Apostrophes are correctly used to form contractions and to show possession.		

Comments: _____

_____

_____

_____

_____

Extra Prompts

1. Pick an outside location, maybe the park, a baseball field, your backyard, etc. In three paragraphs, describe in detail what you hear, see, and smell.

2. Imagine that you have the most unusual pet in the whole town. Describe your pet and what makes it so unusual and unique.

3. Imagine you are an explorer and have just discovered an uncharted island. Describe your discovery so that your friends back home can picture the island in their minds.

4. You've left an important assignment in a shoebox in your closet at home. You are on the phone trying to describe the shoebox to your mom. The problem is that there are five different shoeboxes in your closet. Describe in detail the one shoebox that contains your assignment.

5. Everyone has a favorite outfit. Write a paragraph describing your favorite outfit, from your head to your toes!

6. Your school is having a flag-design contest to select a new school flag. You've decided to enter the contest. Describe in detail what your flag will look like.

7. You and your best friend stumble upon a buried treasure chest. As you open the chest you are amazed at the riches inside! Describe the contents of the chest.

8. You've won the grand prize from Playground Equipment, Inc. This entitles you to any playground setup of your choice. Describe in detail the new equipment for your new playground.

Extra Prompts

9. Write a description of your favorite television show, including the characters, setting, and basic plot of the show.

10. If you had the money to buy any car, what would you choose? Write a descriptive paragraph of your dream car.

11. Flip to any illustration or photograph in a magazine. Write a descriptive paragraph describing the scene.

12. Write a descriptive paragraph about one of the funniest things you've ever seen and why it was so funny to you.

13. Do you like pop? Rock 'n' roll? Jazz? Write a description of your favorite musician or music group. Include a description of the person or group as well as the type of music played.

14. Monopoly®? Scattergories®? Pictionary®? Describe a favorite game you enjoy playing with your family or friends. Be sure to describe the basic object of the game and how a person wins.

15. Have a sweet tooth? Describe your favorite candy bar. Include the main ingredients and describe whether the bar is crunchy, chewy, or gooey.

16. No one knows you better than yourself. Write two descriptive paragraphs about yourself. In the first paragraph, describe your physical characteristics (what you look like). In the second paragraph, describe your personality.

Editing Symbols

Writers use special marks called *editing symbols* to help them edit and revise their work. Editing symbols are used to show what changes a writer wants to make in his or her writing.

Symbol	Meaning	Example
⬯	Correct spelling.	animl
ℓ	Delete or remove.	dogg
◡	Close the gap.	fi sh
∧	Add a letter or word.	lives in tree a
#	Make a space.	fliessouth
∿	Reverse the order of a letter, a word, or words.	plants eats
⩓	Insert a comma.	the crab an arthropod
⊙	Insert a period.	Cats purr
⌄	Insert an apostrophe.	a deers antlers
⌄⌄ ⌄⌄	Insert quotation marks.	She said, Look at the pig.
≡	Make the letter a capital.	birds eat seeds.
/	Make the letter lowercase.	a Snowshoe hare
¶	Start a new paragraph.	Some dogs have tails.